50 Chocolate Lover's Cookbook Recipes

By: Kelly Johnson

Table of Contents

- Classic Chocolate Brownies
- Chocolate Lava Cake
- Chocolate Truffles
- Chocolate Chip Cookies
- Chocolate Mousse
- Chocolate Fondue
- Chocolate Tarts
- Dark Chocolate Ganache Cake
- Hot Chocolate
- Chocolate-Covered Strawberries
- Chocolate Cheesecake
- Chocolate Pudding
- Triple Chocolate Muffins
- Chocolate Fudge
- Chocolate-Dipped Pretzels
- Chocolate Almond Bark
- Chocolate Chip Scones
- Chocolate Ice Cream
- Chocolate Cupcakes with Buttercream Frosting
- Chocolate Soufflé
- Chocolate-Covered Bacon
- Chocolate Mint Brownies
- Chocolate Popcorn
- Mocha Chocolate Cake
- Chocolate-Dipped Coconut Macaroons
- Chocolate Coconut Truffles
- Chocolate Peanut Butter Cups
- Chocolate Banana Bread
- Flourless Chocolate Cake
- Chocolate Panna Cotta
- Chocolate Croissants
- Chocolate Rice Krispies Treats
- Chocolate Hazelnut Spread
- Chocolate Coconut Cake
- Chocolate Cherry Clusters

- Chocolate Granola Bars
- Chocolate Chip Pancakes
- Chocolate Fruit Bark
- White Chocolate Raspberry Cheesecake
- Chocolate Rice Pudding
- Chocolate-Caramel Brownies
- Chocolate Dipped Marshmallows
- Chocolate Ice Cream Sandwiches
- Chocolate Cashew Clusters
- Chocolate Fudge Brownie Ice Cream
- Chocolate Buttercream Frosting
- Chocolate Peanut Butter Pie
- Chocolate S'mores Bars
- Chocolate Zucchini Bread
- Chocolate Milkshakes

Classic Chocolate Brownies

Ingredients:

- 1/2 cup unsalted butter, melted
- 1 cup sugar
- 2 large eggs
- 1 teaspoon vanilla extract
- 1/3 cup unsweetened cocoa powder
- 1/2 cup all-purpose flour
- 1/4 teaspoon salt
- 1/4 teaspoon baking powder

Instructions:

1. Preheat the oven to 350°F (175°C). Grease a 9x9-inch baking pan.
2. In a bowl, mix melted butter, sugar, eggs, and vanilla.
3. Add cocoa powder, flour, salt, and baking powder to the wet ingredients, stirring until combined.
4. Pour the batter into the prepared pan and smooth the top.
5. Bake for 20-25 minutes or until a toothpick comes out clean.
6. Let cool before cutting into squares.

Chocolate Lava Cake

Ingredients:

- 4 oz bittersweet chocolate, chopped
- 1/2 cup unsalted butter
- 1/4 cup powdered sugar
- 2 large eggs
- 2 egg yolks
- 1 teaspoon vanilla extract
- 1/4 cup all-purpose flour

Instructions:

1. Preheat the oven to 425°F (220°C). Grease and flour two ramekins.
2. Melt the chocolate and butter in a microwave or double boiler. Stir in powdered sugar, eggs, egg yolks, and vanilla until smooth.
3. Add flour and stir to combine.
4. Pour the batter into the ramekins, leaving room at the top.
5. Bake for 12-14 minutes, until the edges are set but the center is still soft.
6. Let sit for 1-2 minutes before inverting onto plates. Serve warm.

Chocolate Truffles

Ingredients:

- 8 oz semisweet chocolate, chopped
- 1/2 cup heavy cream
- 1 teaspoon vanilla extract
- Cocoa powder, powdered sugar, or chopped nuts for coating

Instructions:

1. Heat cream in a saucepan over medium heat until simmering.
2. Pour the hot cream over chopped chocolate and stir until smooth.
3. Stir in vanilla extract and chill the mixture for about 1-2 hours, until firm.
4. Shape the mixture into small balls.
5. Roll in cocoa powder, powdered sugar, or chopped nuts.
6. Store in the fridge and serve chilled.

Chocolate Chip Cookies

Ingredients:

- 1 cup unsalted butter, softened
- 3/4 cup white sugar
- 3/4 cup packed brown sugar
- 2 large eggs
- 1 teaspoon vanilla extract
- 2 1/4 cups all-purpose flour
- 1 teaspoon baking soda
- 1/2 teaspoon salt
- 2 cups chocolate chips

Instructions:

1. Preheat the oven to 350°F (175°C). Line baking sheets with parchment paper.
2. Cream butter, white sugar, and brown sugar together until light and fluffy.
3. Beat in eggs and vanilla extract.
4. In a separate bowl, mix flour, baking soda, and salt. Gradually add to the wet ingredients.
5. Stir in chocolate chips.
6. Drop spoonfuls of dough onto the prepared baking sheets.
7. Bake for 10-12 minutes, or until edges are golden. Let cool on a wire rack.

Chocolate Mousse

Ingredients:

- 6 oz dark chocolate, chopped
- 1 cup heavy cream
- 2 tablespoons sugar
- 1 teaspoon vanilla extract
- Whipped cream or berries for garnish

Instructions:

1. Melt the chocolate in a microwave or double boiler. Let cool slightly.
2. Whip the cream and sugar until stiff peaks form.
3. Gently fold the melted chocolate into the whipped cream.
4. Spoon the mousse into serving glasses and refrigerate for at least 2 hours.
5. Garnish with whipped cream or berries before serving.

Chocolate Fondue

Ingredients:

- 8 oz dark chocolate, chopped
- 1/2 cup heavy cream
- 2 tablespoons sugar
- 1 teaspoon vanilla extract
- Fruits, marshmallows, or pound cake for dipping

Instructions:

1. Melt the chocolate and heavy cream in a saucepan over low heat, stirring until smooth.
2. Stir in sugar and vanilla extract.
3. Pour into a fondue pot and keep warm.
4. Serve with fruit, marshmallows, or pound cake for dipping.

Chocolate Tarts

Ingredients:

- 1 pre-made tart crust
- 6 oz semisweet chocolate, chopped
- 1/2 cup heavy cream
- 2 tablespoons sugar
- 1 teaspoon vanilla extract
- Fresh berries for garnish

Instructions:

1. Preheat the oven to 350°F (175°C). Bake the tart crust as per instructions.
2. Heat the heavy cream in a saucepan until simmering. Pour over the chopped chocolate and stir until smooth.
3. Add sugar and vanilla extract. Stir to combine.
4. Pour the chocolate mixture into the baked tart shell.
5. Let cool to room temperature and refrigerate for 2 hours.
6. Garnish with fresh berries before serving.

Dark Chocolate Ganache Cake

Ingredients:

- 1 1/2 cups all-purpose flour
- 1 cup sugar
- 1/2 teaspoon baking powder
- 1/2 teaspoon baking soda
- 1/4 teaspoon salt
- 3/4 cup unsweetened cocoa powder
- 1/2 cup butter, softened
- 2 large eggs
- 1 cup milk
- 1 teaspoon vanilla extract
- 6 oz dark chocolate, chopped
- 1/2 cup heavy cream

Instructions:

1. Preheat the oven to 350°F (175°C). Grease and flour a 9-inch cake pan.
2. In a bowl, whisk together flour, sugar, baking powder, baking soda, salt, and cocoa powder.
3. Add the butter, eggs, milk, and vanilla. Mix until smooth.
4. Pour the batter into the prepared pan and bake for 25-30 minutes. Let cool completely.
5. For ganache, heat heavy cream and pour over chopped chocolate. Stir until smooth.
6. Pour ganache over the cooled cake. Let set before serving.

Hot Chocolate

Ingredients:

- 2 cups milk
- 1/2 cup heavy cream
- 2 oz dark chocolate, chopped
- 2 tablespoons sugar
- 1/2 teaspoon vanilla extract

Instructions:

1. Heat the milk and heavy cream in a saucepan over medium heat until steaming.
2. Add the chocolate and sugar, stirring until melted and smooth.
3. Stir in vanilla extract.
4. Serve warm with whipped cream or marshmallows.

Chocolate-Covered Strawberries

Ingredients:

- 1 pint fresh strawberries, washed and dried
- 8 oz semisweet or dark chocolate, chopped
- 1 tablespoon coconut oil (optional)

Instructions:

1. Melt the chocolate and coconut oil in a microwave or double boiler, stirring until smooth.
2. Dip each strawberry into the melted chocolate, coating it halfway.
3. Place the dipped strawberries on parchment paper to cool and set.
4. Refrigerate for 30 minutes until the chocolate is firm.

Chocolate Cheesecake

Ingredients:

- 1 1/2 cups graham cracker crumbs
- 1/4 cup sugar
- 1/2 cup butter, melted
- 3 (8 oz) packages cream cheese, softened
- 1 cup sugar
- 3 large eggs
- 1/2 cup sour cream
- 8 oz dark chocolate, chopped

Instructions:

1. Preheat the oven to 325°F (165°C).
2. Mix graham cracker crumbs, sugar, and melted butter. Press into the bottom of a springform pan.
3. Beat the cream cheese and sugar until smooth. Add eggs one at a time, mixing after each.
4. Melt the chocolate and stir into the cream cheese mixture. Add sour cream and mix until smooth.
5. Pour the mixture over the crust. Bake for 50-60 minutes until set.
6. Let cool, then refrigerate for 4 hours. Serve chilled.

Chocolate Pudding

Ingredients:

- 2 cups whole milk
- 1/2 cup sugar
- 1/3 cup unsweetened cocoa powder
- 1/4 cup cornstarch
- 1/4 teaspoon salt
- 4 large egg yolks
- 2 tablespoons unsalted butter
- 1 teaspoon vanilla extract

Instructions:

1. In a medium saucepan, whisk together milk, sugar, cocoa powder, cornstarch, and salt.
2. Cook over medium heat, whisking constantly until the mixture thickens and comes to a boil.
3. Remove from heat. Whisk the egg yolks in a separate bowl, then slowly pour a small amount of the hot mixture into the yolks to temper. Gradually whisk the yolks back into the pan.
4. Return to low heat and cook for 2 minutes.
5. Remove from heat, stir in butter and vanilla.
6. Pour into serving bowls and refrigerate for at least 2 hours before serving.

Triple Chocolate Muffins

Ingredients:

- 1 1/2 cups all-purpose flour
- 1 cup sugar
- 1/2 cup unsweetened cocoa powder
- 1 teaspoon baking powder
- 1/2 teaspoon baking soda
- 1/2 teaspoon salt
- 2 large eggs
- 1/2 cup milk
- 1/2 cup vegetable oil
- 1 teaspoon vanilla extract
- 1/2 cup semisweet chocolate chips
- 1/2 cup milk chocolate chips
- 1/2 cup white chocolate chips

Instructions:

1. Preheat the oven to 350°F (175°C) and grease a muffin tin.
2. In a large bowl, whisk together flour, sugar, cocoa powder, baking powder, baking soda, and salt.
3. In another bowl, whisk the eggs, milk, oil, and vanilla.
4. Add the wet ingredients to the dry ingredients and stir until just combined.
5. Gently fold in all the chocolate chips.
6. Fill the muffin tin cups with batter and bake for 18-22 minutes, or until a toothpick inserted comes out clean.
7. Let cool before serving.

Chocolate Fudge

Ingredients:

- 2 cups semisweet chocolate chips
- 1 cup sweetened condensed milk
- 1/4 cup unsalted butter
- 1 teaspoon vanilla extract
- Pinch of salt

Instructions:

1. In a saucepan, melt chocolate chips, sweetened condensed milk, and butter over low heat, stirring constantly.
2. Once melted, remove from heat and stir in vanilla extract and salt.
3. Pour the fudge mixture into a greased 8x8-inch pan and smooth the top.
4. Refrigerate for at least 2 hours until firm.
5. Cut into squares and serve.

Chocolate-Dipped Pretzels

Ingredients:

- 1 cup semisweet chocolate chips
- 1 tablespoon vegetable oil
- Pretzels (mini or regular size)

Instructions:

1. Melt the chocolate chips and vegetable oil together in a heatproof bowl over a double boiler or microwave. Stir until smooth.
2. Dip each pretzel into the melted chocolate, allowing excess to drip off.
3. Place the dipped pretzels on a parchment-lined baking sheet.
4. Chill in the refrigerator for about 30 minutes or until the chocolate is set.
5. Serve and enjoy!

Chocolate Almond Bark

Ingredients:

- 8 oz dark chocolate, chopped
- 1/2 cup almonds, chopped or slivered

Instructions:

1. Melt the dark chocolate in a microwave or double boiler. Stir until smooth.
2. Spread the melted chocolate onto a parchment-lined baking sheet, smoothing it into an even layer.
3. Sprinkle chopped almonds on top of the chocolate.
4. Let the bark cool at room temperature, then refrigerate for 1 hour until fully set.
5. Break into pieces and serve.

Chocolate Chip Scones

Ingredients:

- 2 cups all-purpose flour
- 1/4 cup sugar
- 2 teaspoons baking powder
- 1/4 teaspoon salt
- 1/2 cup unsalted butter, cold and cubed
- 3/4 cup heavy cream
- 1 large egg
- 1 teaspoon vanilla extract
- 1/2 cup chocolate chips

Instructions:

1. Preheat the oven to 400°F (200°C).
2. In a bowl, mix the flour, sugar, baking powder, and salt.
3. Add the cold butter and cut it into the dry ingredients using a pastry cutter or fork until it resembles coarse crumbs.
4. In another bowl, whisk together the cream, egg, and vanilla.
5. Add the wet ingredients to the dry ingredients, mixing gently until just combined.
6. Fold in the chocolate chips.
7. Turn the dough onto a floured surface and shape it into a disc. Cut into wedges and place on a baking sheet.
8. Bake for 15-18 minutes, or until golden brown. Let cool before serving.

Chocolate Ice Cream

Ingredients:

- 2 cups heavy cream
- 1 cup whole milk
- 3/4 cup sugar
- 1/2 cup unsweetened cocoa powder
- 4 large egg yolks
- 1 teaspoon vanilla extract
- 4 oz semisweet chocolate, chopped

Instructions:

1. In a saucepan, heat cream, milk, and sugar until warm.
2. Whisk together the egg yolks in a separate bowl. Gradually add a small amount of the warm cream mixture to the yolks to temper them.
3. Pour the tempered yolks into the saucepan and cook over low heat, stirring constantly until thickened.
4. Remove from heat and stir in the cocoa powder, chopped chocolate, and vanilla extract.
5. Pour the mixture into a bowl and refrigerate for at least 4 hours.
6. Churn the chilled mixture in an ice cream maker according to the manufacturer's instructions.
7. Freeze until firm and serve.

Chocolate Cupcakes with Buttercream Frosting

Ingredients for Cupcakes:

- 1 1/2 cups all-purpose flour
- 3/4 cup cocoa powder
- 1 teaspoon baking powder
- 1/2 teaspoon baking soda
- 1/4 teaspoon salt
- 1/2 cup unsalted butter, softened
- 1 cup sugar
- 2 large eggs
- 1 teaspoon vanilla extract
- 3/4 cup milk

Ingredients for Buttercream Frosting:

- 1/2 cup unsalted butter, softened
- 2 cups powdered sugar
- 2 tablespoons cocoa powder
- 1/4 teaspoon vanilla extract
- 1-2 tablespoons milk

Instructions for Cupcakes:

1. Preheat the oven to 350°F (175°C). Line a muffin tin with cupcake liners.
2. In a bowl, mix the flour, cocoa powder, baking powder, baking soda, and salt.
3. In another bowl, beat the butter and sugar until light and fluffy.
4. Add the eggs and vanilla, beating until smooth.
5. Gradually add the dry ingredients, alternating with the milk.
6. Fill cupcake liners about 2/3 full with batter.
7. Bake for 18-22 minutes, or until a toothpick comes out clean. Let cool completely.

Instructions for Buttercream Frosting:

1. Beat the butter until smooth.
2. Gradually add powdered sugar, cocoa powder, and vanilla.
3. Add milk as needed to reach a spreadable consistency.
4. Frost cooled cupcakes and serve.

Chocolate Soufflé

Ingredients:

- 6 oz semisweet chocolate, chopped
- 1/4 cup unsalted butter
- 3 large eggs, separated
- 1/4 cup sugar
- 1 teaspoon vanilla extract
- Pinch of salt

Instructions:

1. Preheat the oven to 375°F (190°C). Grease and flour two ramekins.
2. Melt the chocolate and butter together in a microwave or double boiler.
3. Beat the egg yolks with sugar until light and fluffy. Stir in the melted chocolate and vanilla.
4. Beat the egg whites with salt until stiff peaks form.
5. Gently fold the egg whites into the chocolate mixture.
6. Pour into prepared ramekins and bake for 12-15 minutes, until risen. Serve immediately.

Chocolate-Covered Bacon

Ingredients:

- 8 slices bacon
- 4 oz semisweet or dark chocolate, chopped
- 1 teaspoon sea salt (optional)

Instructions:

1. Preheat the oven to 375°F (190°C).
2. Lay the bacon slices on a baking sheet and bake for 15-20 minutes, or until crispy.
3. While the bacon cooks, melt the chocolate in a microwave or double boiler.
4. Once the bacon is done, dip each slice into the melted chocolate, coating it halfway.
5. Place the dipped bacon on parchment paper and sprinkle with sea salt if desired.
6. Let the chocolate set at room temperature or refrigerate until firm. Serve and enjoy!

Chocolate Mint Brownies

Ingredients:

- 1/2 cup unsalted butter, melted
- 1 cup sugar
- 2 large eggs
- 1 teaspoon vanilla extract
- 1/2 cup unsweetened cocoa powder
- 1/2 cup all-purpose flour
- 1/4 teaspoon baking powder
- 1/4 teaspoon salt
- 1/2 cup chocolate chips
- 1/4 cup mint chocolate chips (or peppermint extract)

Instructions:

1. Preheat the oven to 350°F (175°C). Grease an 8x8-inch baking pan.
2. In a bowl, mix the melted butter, sugar, eggs, and vanilla extract.
3. Add the cocoa powder, flour, baking powder, and salt. Stir to combine.
4. Fold in the chocolate chips and mint chocolate chips.
5. Pour the batter into the prepared pan and bake for 25-30 minutes, or until a toothpick comes out clean.
6. Let cool before cutting into squares and serving.

Chocolate Popcorn

Ingredients:

- 1/2 cup popcorn kernels
- 1 cup semisweet chocolate chips
- 2 tablespoons unsalted butter
- 1 teaspoon vanilla extract
- 1/4 teaspoon salt

Instructions:

1. Pop the popcorn kernels using your preferred method and place them in a large bowl.
2. In a microwave-safe bowl, melt the chocolate chips and butter together in 30-second intervals, stirring until smooth.
3. Stir in vanilla extract and salt.
4. Pour the melted chocolate over the popcorn and toss to coat evenly.
5. Spread the chocolate-covered popcorn on a parchment-lined baking sheet to cool and harden.
6. Once set, break into pieces and enjoy!

Mocha Chocolate Cake

Ingredients for Cake:

- 1 3/4 cups all-purpose flour
- 1 cup sugar
- 1/2 cup unsweetened cocoa powder
- 1 teaspoon baking powder
- 1 teaspoon baking soda
- 1/2 teaspoon salt
- 1 cup brewed coffee, cooled
- 1/2 cup buttermilk
- 1/2 cup vegetable oil
- 2 large eggs
- 1 teaspoon vanilla extract

Ingredients for Mocha Frosting:

- 1/2 cup unsalted butter, softened
- 3 cups powdered sugar
- 1/4 cup unsweetened cocoa powder
- 1 tablespoon brewed coffee
- 1 teaspoon vanilla extract

Instructions:

1. Preheat the oven to 350°F (175°C). Grease and flour two 9-inch round cake pans.
2. In a large bowl, whisk together flour, sugar, cocoa powder, baking powder, baking soda, and salt.
3. Add the brewed coffee, buttermilk, oil, eggs, and vanilla extract. Mix until smooth.
4. Pour the batter evenly into the prepared pans.
5. Bake for 25-30 minutes, or until a toothpick inserted comes out clean.
6. Let the cakes cool completely.
7. For the frosting, beat butter until smooth. Gradually add powdered sugar and cocoa powder, mixing until smooth.
8. Add brewed coffee and vanilla extract, and continue mixing.
9. Frost the cooled cakes and serve.

Chocolate-Dipped Coconut Macaroons

Ingredients:

- 2 1/2 cups shredded sweetened coconut
- 2/3 cup sweetened condensed milk
- 1/2 teaspoon vanilla extract
- 1/4 teaspoon almond extract (optional)
- 8 oz semisweet chocolate, chopped

Instructions:

1. Preheat the oven to 325°F (163°C) and line a baking sheet with parchment paper.
2. In a bowl, combine shredded coconut, sweetened condensed milk, vanilla extract, and almond extract (if using).
3. Drop spoonfuls of the coconut mixture onto the prepared baking sheet.
4. Bake for 15-20 minutes, or until golden brown.
5. Let the macaroons cool completely.
6. Melt the chocolate in a microwave or double boiler.
7. Dip the cooled macaroons into the melted chocolate and place them back on the parchment paper.
8. Refrigerate until the chocolate hardens. Serve.

Chocolate Coconut Truffles

Ingredients:

- 1 1/2 cups unsweetened shredded coconut
- 1/2 cup sweetened condensed milk
- 8 oz semisweet chocolate, chopped
- 1/4 teaspoon vanilla extract

Instructions:

1. In a bowl, mix together shredded coconut and sweetened condensed milk.
2. Roll the mixture into small balls and place them on a parchment-lined baking sheet.
3. Freeze for at least 30 minutes to firm up.
4. Melt the chocolate in a microwave or double boiler.
5. Dip each coconut ball into the melted chocolate and return to the baking sheet.
6. Let the truffles set in the refrigerator before serving.

Chocolate Peanut Butter Cups

Ingredients:

- 1 cup semisweet chocolate chips
- 1/2 cup creamy peanut butter
- 1/4 cup powdered sugar
- 1/2 teaspoon vanilla extract

Instructions:

1. Line a muffin tin with paper liners.
2. Melt the chocolate chips in a microwave or double boiler, stirring until smooth.
3. Spoon a small amount of melted chocolate into the bottom of each muffin liner and spread evenly.
4. In a separate bowl, mix peanut butter, powdered sugar, and vanilla extract.
5. Spoon a small amount of the peanut butter mixture into each cup, then cover with more melted chocolate.
6. Refrigerate for 1-2 hours until firm. Serve chilled.

Chocolate Banana Bread

Ingredients:

- 2 ripe bananas, mashed
- 1/2 cup sugar
- 1/4 cup unsalted butter, softened
- 2 large eggs
- 1 teaspoon vanilla extract
- 1 1/2 cups all-purpose flour
- 1 teaspoon baking soda
- 1/2 teaspoon salt
- 1/2 cup semisweet chocolate chips

Instructions:

1. Preheat the oven to 350°F (175°C). Grease a loaf pan.
2. In a bowl, mix the mashed bananas, sugar, butter, eggs, and vanilla extract.
3. Add the flour, baking soda, and salt, and mix until combined.
4. Fold in the chocolate chips.
5. Pour the batter into the prepared loaf pan.
6. Bake for 60-70 minutes, or until a toothpick comes out clean.
7. Let the bread cool before slicing.

Flourless Chocolate Cake

Ingredients:

- 1/2 cup unsalted butter
- 8 oz semisweet chocolate, chopped
- 3/4 cup sugar
- 1/4 teaspoon salt
- 4 large eggs, beaten
- 1 teaspoon vanilla extract

Instructions:

1. Preheat the oven to 375°F (190°C). Grease a 9-inch round cake pan.
2. Melt the butter and chocolate together in a microwave or double boiler. Stir until smooth.
3. Add sugar and salt, mixing well.
4. Stir in the eggs and vanilla extract.
5. Pour the batter into the prepared pan.
6. Bake for 20-25 minutes, or until the cake has set but still slightly moist in the center.
7. Let cool in the pan for 10 minutes, then invert onto a plate and let cool completely. Serve.

Chocolate Panna Cotta

Ingredients:

- 1 1/2 cups heavy cream
- 1/2 cup whole milk
- 1/4 cup sugar
- 2 tablespoons unsweetened cocoa powder
- 1/2 teaspoon vanilla extract
- 2 teaspoons unflavored gelatin

Instructions:

1. In a saucepan, combine the heavy cream, milk, sugar, and cocoa powder.
2. Heat over medium heat until warm but not boiling.
3. Sprinkle the gelatin over the mixture and stir until dissolved.
4. Remove from heat and stir in vanilla extract.
5. Pour the mixture into serving glasses and refrigerate for at least 4 hours until set.
6. Serve chilled, optionally with whipped cream.

Chocolate Croissants

Ingredients:

- 1 package puff pastry, thawed
- 1/2 cup semisweet chocolate chips
- 1 egg, beaten (for egg wash)

Instructions:

1. Preheat the oven to 400°F (200°C).
2. Unfold the puff pastry sheets and cut each into triangles.
3. Place a few chocolate chips in the center of each triangle.
4. Roll the triangles up into croissant shapes and place on a baking sheet.
5. Brush with the beaten egg for a golden finish.
6. Bake for 15-20 minutes, or until puffed and golden.
7. Serve warm.

Chocolate Rice Krispies Treats

Ingredients:

- 6 cups Rice Krispies cereal
- 1/4 cup unsalted butter
- 10 oz marshmallows
- 1/4 cup semisweet chocolate chips

Instructions:

1. In a large saucepan, melt butter over medium heat.
2. Add the marshmallows and stir until completely melted and smooth.
3. Remove from heat and stir in Rice Krispies cereal until evenly coated.
4. Press the mixture into a greased 9x13-inch pan.
5. In a microwave-safe bowl, melt the chocolate chips in 30-second intervals, stirring until smooth.
6. Drizzle the melted chocolate over the Rice Krispies treats.
7. Let cool before cutting into squares.

Chocolate Hazelnut Spread

Ingredients:

- 1 cup hazelnuts, toasted and skins removed
- 1/2 cup semisweet chocolate chips
- 1/4 cup powdered sugar
- 1 tablespoon cocoa powder
- 1/4 teaspoon vanilla extract
- 1-2 tablespoons vegetable oil

Instructions:

1. In a food processor, blend the toasted hazelnuts until they form a paste.
2. Melt the chocolate chips in the microwave or over a double boiler.
3. Add the melted chocolate, powdered sugar, cocoa powder, vanilla extract, and 1 tablespoon oil to the hazelnut paste and blend until smooth.
4. If the spread is too thick, add additional oil, a little at a time, to reach the desired consistency.
5. Store in an airtight container.

Chocolate Coconut Cake

Ingredients for Cake:

- 1 1/2 cups all-purpose flour
- 1 cup sugar
- 1/2 cup unsweetened cocoa powder
- 1 teaspoon baking powder
- 1 teaspoon baking soda
- 1/2 teaspoon salt
- 1/2 cup buttermilk
- 2 large eggs
- 1/2 cup vegetable oil
- 1 teaspoon vanilla extract
- 1 cup boiling water

Ingredients for Frosting:

- 1/2 cup unsalted butter, softened
- 1/2 cup heavy cream
- 1 1/2 cups powdered sugar
- 1/2 cup shredded coconut

Instructions:

1. Preheat the oven to 350°F (175°C) and grease and flour two 9-inch cake pans.
2. In a large bowl, mix together the flour, sugar, cocoa powder, baking powder, baking soda, and salt.
3. Add the buttermilk, eggs, oil, and vanilla extract, and mix until smooth.
4. Gradually stir in the boiling water until the batter is thin.
5. Pour the batter into the prepared pans and bake for 25-30 minutes.
6. While the cake cools, make the frosting by heating the butter and heavy cream in a saucepan.
7. Stir in powdered sugar until smooth.
8. Frost the cooled cake with the frosting and sprinkle shredded coconut on top.

Chocolate Cherry Clusters

Ingredients:

- 1 cup semisweet chocolate chips
- 1/2 cup dried cherries
- 1/2 cup almonds, chopped (optional)

Instructions:

1. In a microwave-safe bowl, melt the chocolate chips in 30-second intervals, stirring until smooth.
2. Stir in dried cherries and chopped almonds, if using.
3. Drop spoonfuls of the chocolate mixture onto a parchment-lined baking sheet.
4. Let the clusters cool and harden in the refrigerator for 1-2 hours.
5. Enjoy chilled.

Chocolate Granola Bars

Ingredients:

- 2 cups rolled oats
- 1/2 cup honey
- 1/2 cup peanut butter
- 1/4 cup semisweet chocolate chips
- 1/4 cup dried fruit (raisins, cranberries)
- 1/4 cup nuts (almonds, walnuts), chopped

Instructions:

1. In a saucepan, heat honey and peanut butter over medium heat until melted and smooth.
2. In a bowl, combine oats, chocolate chips, dried fruit, and chopped nuts.
3. Pour the peanut butter mixture over the oat mixture and stir until well combined.
4. Press the mixture into a greased 8x8-inch pan.
5. Refrigerate for 2 hours to set.
6. Cut into bars and serve.

Chocolate Chip Pancakes

Ingredients:

- 1 cup all-purpose flour
- 1 tablespoon sugar
- 1 teaspoon baking powder
- 1/4 teaspoon baking soda
- 1/4 teaspoon salt
- 3/4 cup milk
- 1 large egg
- 2 tablespoons melted butter
- 1/2 cup chocolate chips

Instructions:

1. In a bowl, mix the flour, sugar, baking powder, baking soda, and salt.
2. In another bowl, whisk together the milk, egg, and melted butter.
3. Add the wet ingredients to the dry ingredients and stir until just combined.
4. Fold in the chocolate chips.
5. Heat a griddle or skillet over medium heat and lightly grease.
6. Pour 1/4 cup of batter onto the griddle for each pancake.
7. Cook for 2-3 minutes on each side, until golden brown.
8. Serve warm with syrup.

Chocolate Fruit Bark

Ingredients:

- 8 oz semisweet chocolate, chopped
- 1/4 cup dried fruit (raisins, cranberries, apricots), chopped
- 1/4 cup nuts (almonds, walnuts), chopped
- 1/4 cup seeds (pumpkin, sunflower)

Instructions:

1. Melt the chocolate in a microwave-safe bowl, stirring every 30 seconds until smooth.
2. Line a baking sheet with parchment paper.
3. Pour the melted chocolate onto the sheet and spread into an even layer.
4. Sprinkle the dried fruit, nuts, and seeds over the melted chocolate.
5. Refrigerate for 1-2 hours until set.
6. Break into pieces and serve.

White Chocolate Raspberry Cheesecake

Ingredients for Crust:

- 1 1/2 cups graham cracker crumbs
- 1/4 cup sugar
- 1/4 cup melted butter

Ingredients for Filling:

- 2 cups cream cheese, softened
- 1/2 cup sugar
- 2 large eggs
- 1 teaspoon vanilla extract
- 1/2 cup white chocolate chips, melted
- 1/2 cup raspberry puree (fresh or frozen raspberries blended)

Instructions:

1. Preheat the oven to 325°F (163°C). Grease a 9-inch springform pan.
2. For the crust, combine graham cracker crumbs, sugar, and melted butter. Press into the bottom of the pan.
3. In a bowl, beat cream cheese, sugar, eggs, and vanilla until smooth.
4. Stir in the melted white chocolate.
5. Pour the filling into the prepared crust.
6. Drizzle the raspberry puree on top and swirl with a knife.
7. Bake for 50-60 minutes, or until set.
8. Let cool before refrigerating for 3 hours.
9. Serve chilled.

Chocolate Rice Pudding

Ingredients:

- 1 cup arborio rice
- 2 cups milk
- 1/2 cup heavy cream
- 1/4 cup sugar
- 1/4 cup semisweet chocolate chips
- 1 teaspoon vanilla extract

Instructions:

1. In a saucepan, combine the rice, milk, cream, and sugar.
2. Cook over medium heat, stirring occasionally, for 20-25 minutes until the rice is tender.
3. Stir in the chocolate chips and vanilla extract, and cook until the chocolate melts.
4. Serve warm or chilled.

Chocolate-Caramel Brownies

Ingredients for Brownies:

- 1/2 cup unsalted butter
- 1 cup sugar
- 2 large eggs
- 1 teaspoon vanilla extract
- 1/2 cup unsweetened cocoa powder
- 1/2 cup all-purpose flour
- 1/4 teaspoon salt

Ingredients for Caramel Sauce:

- 1/2 cup heavy cream
- 1/4 cup unsalted butter
- 1/2 cup brown sugar
- 1 teaspoon vanilla extract

Instructions:

1. Preheat the oven to 350°F (175°C) and grease a 9x9-inch baking pan.
2. For the brownies, melt the butter in a bowl. Stir in sugar, eggs, and vanilla. Add cocoa powder, flour, and salt.
3. Pour the brownie batter into the prepared pan and bake for 20-25 minutes.
4. For the caramel sauce, heat heavy cream, butter, and brown sugar in a saucepan over medium heat.
5. Stir constantly until the caramel thickens.
6. Pour the caramel sauce over the warm brownies.
7. Let cool before cutting into squares.

Chocolate Dipped Marshmallows

Ingredients:

- 12 large marshmallows
- 1 cup semisweet chocolate chips
- 1 tablespoon vegetable oil (optional)
- Sprinkles or crushed nuts (optional)

Instructions:

1. Insert wooden skewers or lollipop sticks into each marshmallow.
2. In a microwave-safe bowl, melt the chocolate chips with vegetable oil (if using) in 30-second intervals, stirring until smooth.
3. Dip each marshmallow into the melted chocolate, ensuring it's fully coated.
4. If desired, roll the chocolate-covered marshmallows in sprinkles or crushed nuts.
5. Place the dipped marshmallows on parchment paper to set. Let cool for 30 minutes.

Chocolate Ice Cream Sandwiches

Ingredients for Cookies:

- 1 1/2 cups all-purpose flour
- 1/2 cup cocoa powder
- 1/2 teaspoon baking soda
- 1/4 teaspoon salt
- 1/2 cup unsalted butter, softened
- 1 cup sugar
- 1 large egg
- 1 teaspoon vanilla extract

Ingredients for Filling:

- 2 cups chocolate ice cream, softened

Instructions:

1. Preheat the oven to 350°F (175°C). Grease or line a baking sheet with parchment paper.
2. In a bowl, mix together flour, cocoa powder, baking soda, and salt.
3. In a separate bowl, cream the butter and sugar until fluffy. Add the egg and vanilla extract, mixing well.
4. Gradually add the dry ingredients to the wet ingredients, mixing until combined.
5. Roll the dough into balls and flatten them into circles. Place them on the baking sheet and bake for 10-12 minutes.
6. Allow cookies to cool completely.
7. Once cooled, spread softened chocolate ice cream on the bottom of one cookie and top with another. Press gently to sandwich them together. Freeze for 1 hour before serving.

Chocolate Cashew Clusters

Ingredients:

- 1 cup semisweet chocolate chips
- 1 cup salted cashews, chopped
- 1/4 cup dried cranberries (optional)

Instructions:

1. Melt the chocolate chips in a microwave-safe bowl, stirring every 30 seconds until smooth.
2. Stir in the chopped cashews and dried cranberries.
3. Drop spoonfuls of the mixture onto a parchment-lined baking sheet.
4. Refrigerate for 1-2 hours to set.
5. Enjoy chilled.

Chocolate Fudge Brownie Ice Cream

Ingredients:

- 2 cups heavy cream
- 1 cup whole milk
- 3/4 cup sugar
- 1 teaspoon vanilla extract
- 1/2 cup semisweet chocolate chips
- 1/2 cup brownie pieces (baked and crumbled)

Instructions:

1. In a saucepan, heat the cream, milk, and sugar over medium heat until the sugar dissolves.
2. Stir in the chocolate chips and heat until melted and smooth.
3. Remove from heat and stir in the vanilla extract.
4. Pour the mixture into an ice cream maker and churn according to the manufacturer's instructions.
5. During the last few minutes of churning, add in the brownie pieces.
6. Transfer the ice cream to a container and freeze for 4-6 hours before serving.

Chocolate Buttercream Frosting

Ingredients:

- 1 cup unsalted butter, softened
- 3 cups powdered sugar
- 1/2 cup unsweetened cocoa powder
- 1 teaspoon vanilla extract
- 2 tablespoons heavy cream (or more, as needed)

Instructions:

1. Beat the softened butter until smooth and creamy.
2. Gradually add the powdered sugar and cocoa powder, beating on low until incorporated.
3. Add vanilla extract and heavy cream, and beat on high until smooth and fluffy.
4. If the frosting is too thick, add more cream, one tablespoon at a time, until the desired consistency is reached.
5. Use to frost cakes, cupcakes, or cookies.

Chocolate Peanut Butter Pie

Ingredients for Crust:

- 1 1/2 cups graham cracker crumbs
- 1/4 cup sugar
- 1/2 cup unsalted butter, melted

Ingredients for Filling:

- 1 cup creamy peanut butter
- 1/2 cup powdered sugar
- 8 oz cream cheese, softened
- 1 cup heavy cream
- 1/2 cup semisweet chocolate chips, melted

Instructions:

1. Preheat the oven to 350°F (175°C).
2. Combine the graham cracker crumbs, sugar, and melted butter. Press the mixture into the bottom of a pie dish and bake for 10 minutes. Let cool.
3. For the filling, beat the peanut butter, powdered sugar, and cream cheese together until smooth.
4. In a separate bowl, whip the heavy cream until stiff peaks form.
5. Fold the whipped cream into the peanut butter mixture and pour into the cooled crust.
6. Drizzle the melted chocolate over the top and swirl it into the filling.
7. Refrigerate for at least 4 hours before serving.

Chocolate S'mores Bars

Ingredients:

- 1 1/2 cups graham cracker crumbs
- 1/4 cup sugar
- 1/2 cup unsalted butter, melted
- 1 1/2 cups semisweet chocolate chips
- 2 cups mini marshmallows

Instructions:

1. Preheat the oven to 350°F (175°C). Grease an 8x8-inch baking dish.
2. Combine graham cracker crumbs, sugar, and melted butter. Press the mixture into the bottom of the baking dish.
3. Bake for 5-7 minutes, then remove from the oven.
4. Sprinkle chocolate chips over the crust, then top with mini marshmallows.
5. Bake for an additional 5-7 minutes, until the marshmallows are golden brown.
6. Let cool before cutting into bars.

Chocolate Zucchini Bread

Ingredients:

- 1 1/2 cups all-purpose flour
- 1/2 cup cocoa powder
- 1/2 teaspoon baking soda
- 1/4 teaspoon baking powder
- 1/2 teaspoon salt
- 1 teaspoon cinnamon
- 2 large eggs
- 1/2 cup sugar
- 1/2 cup vegetable oil
- 1 teaspoon vanilla extract
- 2 cups shredded zucchini (squeezed dry)
- 1/2 cup semisweet chocolate chips

Instructions:

1. Preheat the oven to 350°F (175°C) and grease a loaf pan.
2. In a bowl, whisk together the flour, cocoa powder, baking soda, baking powder, salt, and cinnamon.
3. In a separate bowl, beat the eggs, sugar, oil, and vanilla.
4. Add the dry ingredients to the wet ingredients, mixing until just combined.
5. Stir in the shredded zucchini and chocolate chips.
6. Pour the batter into the loaf pan and bake for 50-60 minutes, or until a toothpick inserted into the center comes out clean.
7. Let cool before slicing.

Chocolate Milkshakes

Ingredients:

- 2 cups vanilla ice cream
- 1/2 cup milk
- 1/4 cup chocolate syrup
- Whipped cream (optional)

Instructions:

1. Blend together the ice cream, milk, and chocolate syrup until smooth.
2. Pour into glasses and top with whipped cream, if desired.
3. Serve immediately with a straw.

www.ingramcontent.com/pod-product-compliance
Lightning Source LLC
LaVergne TN
LVHW081333060526
838201LV00055B/2615